eat smart

Cereals

Vic Parker

Quarto
Knows

Quarto is the authority on a wide range of topics.

Quarto educates, entertains and enriches the lives of
our readers—enthusiasts and lovers of hands-on living.

www.quartoknows.com

Ask an adult for help

Always ask an adult to help you make the recipes and get all the ingredients and equipment ready. Remember to wash your hands before you start.

Publisher: Maxime Boucknooghe
Editorial Director: Victoria Garrard
Art Director: Miranda Snow
Design and Editorial: Starry Dog Books Ltd
Consultant: Charlotte Stirling-Reed BSc (hons), MSc, RNutr (Public Health)

Picture credits
(t=top, b=bottom,
l=left, r=right, c=centre,
fc=front cover)

Alamy fc Keith Leighton / Alamy Stock Photo, 8cl Keith Leighton

Corbis 21t Scott Sinklier

Dreamstime 21br Andy St John

Getty Images 21bl Stone/PBJ Pictures

Shutterstock fc PetrP, fc Jim Parkin, fc Richard Griffin, fc russ witherington, fc Viktor1, fc Sheli Jensen, fc AlenKadr, fc Evgeny Karandaev, fc alisafarov, 4tl Tomo Jesenicnik, 4tr PetrP, 4bl Jim Parkin, 4bc PetrP, 4br Anbk, 5 Alessio Ponti, 6c Jim Parkin, 6bc Microgen, 6–7 Martine Oger, 7tl PetrP, 7tr PetrP, 7cr Tomo Jesenicnik, 7bl Fotohunter, 7br Anbk, fc PetrP, 8tl V J Matthew, 8tr Ericsmandes, 8bl Joe Gough, fc Fanfo, 8br Gelpi, 9tr Matka Wariatka, 9cl (oat cookie) Igor Kovalchuk, 9c Viktor1 (pasta), 9bl Russ Witherington, 9bc (carrot cake) Nataliya Arzamasova, 9br Fanfo, 11r Robert Milek, 11l Konstantin Remizov, 12tr Anbk, 12cl Stanislav Komogorov, 12bl Mosista Pambudi, 12br Mosista Pambudi, 13t huyangshu, 13c Digital Shuts, 13bl Lesya Dolyuk, 15tr Hallgerd, 15br Hallgerd, 16cl Bruce Works, 16cr Alexander Briel Perez, 16bl Orientaly, 17tl Sarah Johnson, 17cr Dusan Po, 17bl Ints Vikmanis, 17br Rozaliya, 19br russ witherington, 20tr Jim Parkin, 20cl Noam Armonn, 20cr David Hughes, 20br N. Mitchell, 21cr Woudew.

Public domain
17bc, 21br

Words in **bold** are explained in the glossary on page 22.

Contents

Cereal plants

Cereal plants produce **grains**. The grains are the seeds of the plants. They are used to make foods.

Wheat

Oats

Maize

There are many different types of cereal, such as wheat, oats, rice, barley and maize.

Rice

Barley

The cluster, or group, of grains on a wheat plant is called an ear.

Cereal plants shoot up as tall grasses with the grains at the top. More cereal plants are grown than any other type of **crop**.

You will need:

- 2 tbsp wheat grains
- A jam jar
- Spring water
- A piece of **muslin** (thin cloth)
- An elastic band

Grow a wheat plant

1 Put the wheat grains into the jam jar. Cover the grains with spring water.

2 Place the muslin over the jar and secure it with an elastic band. Put the jar in a warm place. Leave overnight.

3 The next day, drain the water out through the muslin. Rinse the grains with fresh spring water and drain again, leaving the grains just moist. Repeat twice a day.

4 In a few days, the grains will start to sprout.

5

Cereals around the world

Different types of cereals are grown around the world.

Cereals need the right conditions in order to grow. Some cereals need lots of rain. Others prefer the soil to be dry.

North America

South America

Maize plants grow well in warm weather and damp soil. The United States of America produces nearly half of the world's maize.

Quinoa (say *keen-wah*) grows well in the mountains of Peru in South America.

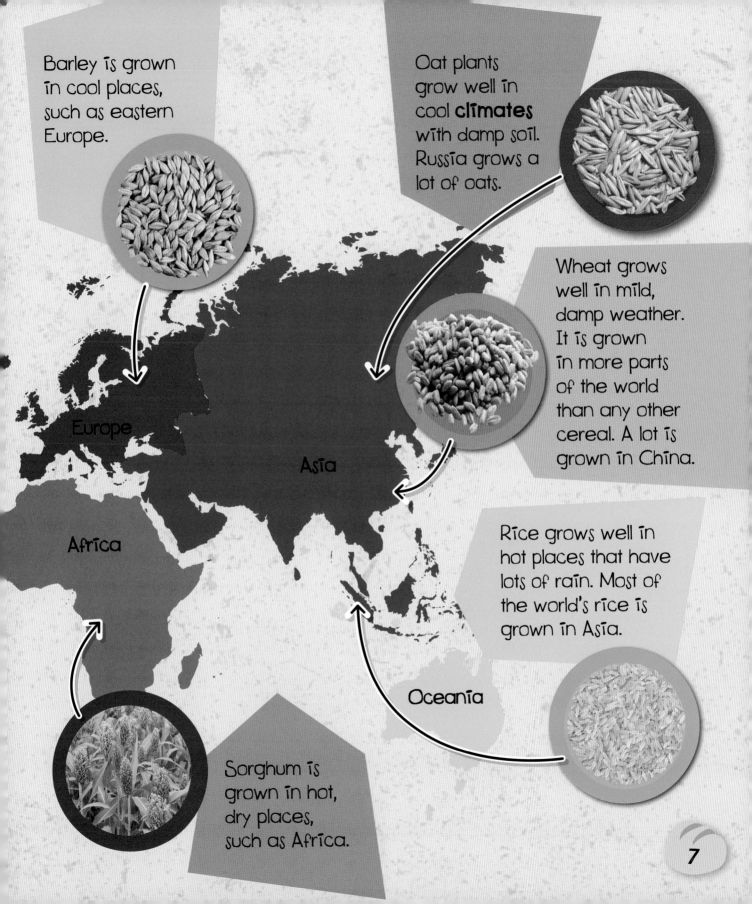

Barley is grown in cool places, such as eastern Europe.

Oat plants grow well in cool **climates** with damp soil. Russia grows a lot of oats.

Wheat grows well in mild, damp weather. It is grown in more parts of the world than any other cereal. A lot is grown in China.

Rice grows well in hot places that have lots of rain. Most of the world's rice is grown in Asia.

Sorghum is grown in hot, dry places, such as Africa.

Europe

Asia

Africa

Oceania

Cereals in meals

Cereals make up a large part of the food we eat each day.

In the afternoon we might snack on a rice cake with fruit.

In the morning we might eat a breakfast cereal, or some oats.

For lunch we might have couscous with red peppers.

For dinner we could have rice with a chicken curry.

8

Ingredients:

- 150 ml skimmed milk or almond milk (use less for a thicker smoothie)
- 2 small bananas
- 500 g frozen berries
- 50 g wheatgerm
- 4 ice cubes

Makes: 1 to 2 servings

Make a wheatgerm smoothie

1 Put the milk, fruit and wheatgerm into a blender and blend for one minute.

2 Add the ice cubes and blend for another 30 seconds.

3 Pour into glasses and serve.

Cookie

Many of the foods we eat, such as pizza and pasta, are made from flour. Flour is made by grinding up grains from cereals such as wheat, rice or sorghum.

Bread

Pasta

Cake

Pizza

Cereals for a healthy body

Cereals contain **carbohydrates** and lots of other nutrients. They should make up a third of all the food we eat.

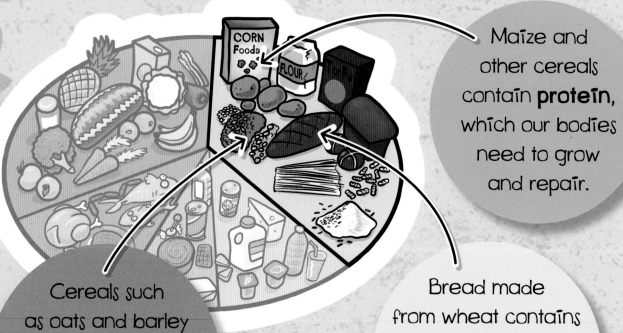

Maize and other cereals contain **protein**, which our bodies need to grow and repair.

Cereals such as oats and barley contain soluble **fibre**, which helps to keep our digestive system healthy.

Bread made from wheat contains B vitamins, which help our bodies to release energy from food.

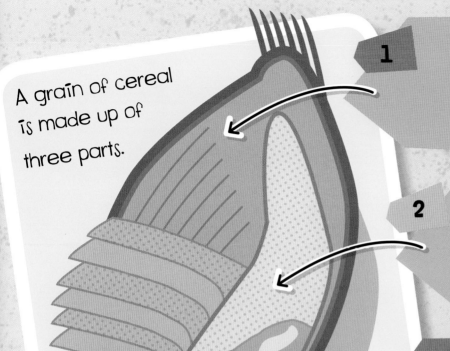

A grain of cereal is made up of three parts.

1 The outer layer is called bran. It is mainly fibre.

2 The largest inner part is called the endosperm. It is mainly carbohydrate.

3 The smallest inner part is called the germ. It is rich in protein.

Food facts

White flour is made from a grain's endosperm. It is used to make white bread. Wholemeal flour is used to make brown bread. It is made from whole grains, so it contains more fibre and nutrients.

White bread

Brown bread

Growing rice

Rice

Rice grows best in hot countries, and needs lots of water to grow.

1 The seeds are planted and sprout in seedbeds that are flooded with water.

Young rice plants are moved to larger flooded fields called paddies. There, they grow in water about 12 centimetres deep.

2

3 The plants grow for three to five months. Then they are ready for **harvesting**.

4 Some farmers tie the stems into bundles and cut them by hand. Then they beat them against bamboo to separate the grains.

Other farmers drain the fields and use machines to harvest the rice.

5

Ingredients:

- 8 tbsp honey
- 120 g almond butter or unsalted peanut butter
- 100 g puffed rice cereal
- 25 g chocolate

Makes: 16 squares

Make a puffed rice treat

1 Put the honey into a saucepan. Ask an adult to boil it for one minute. Remove the pan from the heat and stir in the nut butter.

2 Add the puffed rice cereal. Stir well until all the rice is coated. Tip the mixture into a tray lined with baking paper and press it down. Leave to cool.

3 Ask an adult to melt the chocolate. Drizzle it over the mixture.

4 Put in the fridge until the chocolate has gone hard, then serve.

Make vegetable fried rice

Ingredients:

- 110 g white, long grain rice
- 2 tsp sesame oil
- 1 red pepper, chopped
- 10 baby corns
- 6 mushrooms, chopped

Makes: 2 servings

Try using rice to make a healthy and tasty dish.

Put the rice into a sieve and rinse it well with cold water.

1

2

Tip the rice into a saucepan and cover it with water. Ask an adult to cook the rice on a low heat for about 10 minutes.

3 Ask an adult to heat the oil in a frying pan and help you fry the vegetables for five minutes.

Basmati rice

Food fact

There are more than 40,000 types of rice grown all over the world.

4 Add the cooked rice to the frying pan. Stir and serve straight away.

Wild rice

Growing wheat

Wheat grows quickest on warm, wet days. But it needs sunshine to ripen.

1 Young wheat looks like grass. In cold weather, the plants grow slowly.

As the weather warms up, the plants grow faster. **2**

3 Ripe wheat is golden. Combine harvesters pull the ears from the stems and separate the grains.

4 The grains are then turned into foods such as breakfast cereals and flour.

The dry, dead wheat stalks are called straw. They are bundled into large bales.

5

6 The straw is used as food and bedding for animals.

Food fact

In the United States, wheat is grown in 42 out of the 50 states.

Bake bread

A lot of wheat flour is used to make bread. Try baking some bread of your own with this easy recipe.

1 Put the flour, sugar, salt and margarine into a bowl and mix them together.

2 Add the yeast and water, and stir well. Use your hands to shape the dough into a ball.

18

Push and stretch the dough for about 10 minutes until it feels soft and smooth. This is called kneading.

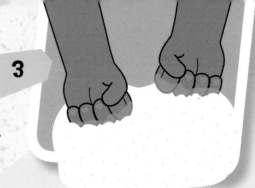

3

Put the dough onto a greased baking tray. Cover it with greased cling film and put it in a warm place.

4

Leave the dough for 30 minutes – it should double in size. While it is rising, ask an adult to set the oven to 230°C/450°F/Gas 8.

5

6

Remove the cling film and ask an adult to put the tray into the oven. Bake for 25 minutes until the bread is golden brown.

Growing maize

Maize

There are many different types of maize. Sweetcorn is one variety.

These people are planting sweetcorn seedlings in rows.

The young shoots soon grow into tall stalks. The stalks develop ears, or cobs, of sweetcorn.

Long, silky threads grow out of the cobs. When these turn brown, it's almost harvest time.

4 A full-grown sweetcorn plant can be up to 1.8 metres tall.

Combine harvesters pull the cobs off the stems and separate the grains. The grains are tinned or frozen in factories. **5**

6 Sometimes farmers sell whole cobs of sweetcorn to shops, where we can buy them to eat.

Food fact

You can eat baby corns raw in salads. They are also often cooked in vegetable stir-fries.

Glossary

Carbohydrates
Foods that contain sugar and starch, which give us energy.

Climate
The typical weather of a certain area.

Crop
A plant grown in large amounts to be eaten or used by people or animals.

Fibre
Fibre is the part of plants that our bodies cannot digest. There are two types of fibre – insoluble and soluble. Both types are important for a healthy, balanced diet. Insoluble fibre makes it easier for our bodies to get rid of waste food. Soluble fibre helps to keep our digestive system healthy.

Grains
The tiny, dry seeds of a cereal plant.

Harvesting
Gathering or collecting crops from a field.

Muslin
A very fine cotton fabric.

Protein
A substance in foods that helps the body to grow and repair itself.